Celebrate *the* Century

A COLLECTION OF COMMEMORATIVE STAMPS

1900-1909

PUT YOUR STAMP ON HISTORY
1900 · 2000

UNITED STATES
POSTAL SERVICE™

UNITED STATES POSTAL SERVICE

POSTMASTER GENERAL
AND CHIEF EXECUTIVE OFFICER
Marvin Runyon

CHIEF MARKETING OFFICER AND
SENIOR VICE PRESIDENT
Allen Kane

EXECUTIVE DIRECTOR, STAMP SERVICES
Azeezaly S. Jaffer

MANAGER, STAMP MARKETING
Valoree Vargo

PROJECT MANAGER
Gary A. Thuro Jr.

TIME-LIFE BOOKS IS A DIVISION OF TIME LIFE INC.

TIME-LIFE CUSTOM PUBLISHING

VICE PRESIDENT AND PUBLISHER
Terry Newell

VICE PRESIDENT OF
NEW BUSINESS DEVELOPMENT
Michael A. Hurley

DIRECTOR OF EDITORIAL DEVELOPMENT
Jennifer Louise Pearce

CUSTOM MARKETING MANAGER
John Charles Loyack

EDITORIAL STAFF FOR CELEBRATE THE CENTURY

MANAGING EDITOR
Morin Bishop

EDITORS
Sally Guard, John Bolster

DESIGNER
Barbara Chilenskas

WRITERS
Merrell Noden, Eve Peterson

RESEARCHERS
*Jenny Douglas,
Jessica Goldstein, Lauren Cardonsky*

PHOTO EDITOR
Bill Broyles

First printing. Printed in U.S.A.

TIME-LIFE is a trademark of Time Warner Inc. U.S.A.

LIBRARY OF CONGRESS CATALOGING-IN-PUBLICATION DATA
Celebrate the century: a collection of commemorative stamps.
p.   cm.   Includes index.
Contents: v. 1. 1900–1909
ISBN 0-7835-5317-X
1. Commemorative postage stamps—United States—History—20th century.
2. United States—History—20th century.
I. Time-Life Books

HE6185.U5C45 1998   97–46952
769.56973—DC21   CIP

Books produced by Time-Life Custom Publishing are available at a special bulk discount for promotional and premium use. Custom adaptations can also be created to meet your specific marketing goals. Call 1-800-323-5255.

PICTURE CREDITS

CONTENTS

Introduction
4

THE ASH CAN ARTISTS
10

THEODORE ROOSEVELT
16

ELLIS ISLAND
22

THE GIBSON GIRL
28

THE GREAT TRAIN ROBBERY
32

MODEL T
38

JOHN MUIR
44

PURE FOOD AND DRUGS ACT
50

CRAYOLA CRAYONS
56

W.E.B. DU BOIS
60

KITTY HAWK
66

THE ROBIE HOUSE
72

ST. LOUIS WORLD'S FAIR
78

TEDDY BEAR
84

THE WORLD SERIES®
90

Index
96

The new century found expression in the optimism of the World's Fair (left) and the ingenuity of the Model T (above).

INTRODUCTION

The first decade of the twentieth century was a period of intense self-scrutiny for Americans, a time to pause amid the dizzying rush of technology and industry and ask themselves if they liked the nation they had become. To most, it seemed a Dickensian decade, the best and the worst of times.

Certainly, it was a period of tremendous prosperity. "Furnaces are glowing, spindles are singing their song," boasted Mark Hanna, the senator from Ohio. "Happiness comes to us all with prosperity." The St. Louis World's Fair of 1904, which attracted some 20 million avid attendees in its seven months, was a great, gawdy paean to progress. Of course, one didn't have to go to St. Louis to know that momentous changes were taking place. Everywhere one looked, on the

land and in the sky, there was proof of human ingenuity. In December 1903, just months before the Fair opened, on a windy stretch of beach at Kitty Hawk, North Carolina, the Wright Brothers had piloted their 12-horsepower biplane on a series of wobbly flights, the longest of which lasted 59 seconds and covered 852 feet. That same year Henry Ford, who had designed his first motorcar in 1896, formed the Ford Motor Company to build what even he initially assumed would be a toy for the rich. But in 1908 Ford began mass-producing the Model T with the help of an assembly line, and in so doing steered the modern world in a whole new direction. Overnight, the price of a motorcar plummeted, from $5,000 to $850. By 1916, it had fallen even further, to $360, a sum within reach of middle-class Americans. Safe and

The advent of the airplane further bolstered the belief that technology could master any challenge.

reliable, Ford's Model T transformed the nation, bringing the farm and the city closer together, showing the way for more productive factory layouts, and bestowing on ordinary people an unprecedented measure of mobility and freedom.

It was hard not to view these mind-boggling technological advances as proof that the world was improving and that the future would be a richer, more comfortable, better place to live. Still, when Americans looked in the mirror, they were troubled by what they saw. Were the horrific slums so forcefully depicted by New York City's Ashcan Artists mere growing pains, soon to yield to the march of progress? Or were they something darker, proof that the United States had lost its way, betrayed the principles of fairness and equality that had made it great?

The United States had been growing at a frenetic pace, gobbling up vast tracts of land in the West until the 45 states that comprised the country in 1900 truly stretched from sea to shining sea. In the previous 50 years the population had nearly tripled, to just under 76 million. Immigrants were pouring through Ellis Island and other ports of entry; cities were filling up so fast that neither housing nor sewage lines could keep pace; industry was booming and corporations were becoming conglomerates.

A lucky few had taken advantage of this growth and prospered mightily, but many more had suffered in the prevailing atmosphere of anything-goes greed and exploitation. In the increasingly settled but still wild West, cattlemen and rogue miners were busy pillaging wilderness areas that were national treasures. Factory workers were wage slaves, forced to put in cruelly long hours in horrendous conditions, as Upton Sinclair revealed in his novel of the Chicago stockyards, *The Jungle*. Lowest on the ladder of exploitation were African-Americans who, though technically

The millions of immigrants who came to America found a hopeful nation but one beset with problems too.

free of slavery, still suffered disproportionately. W.E.B. Du Bois, who in 1895 had become the first African-American to earn a Ph.D. from Harvard, cofounded the National Association for the Advancement of Colored People in 1909, envisioning it as a more radical alternative to the ideals of Booker T. Washington, who was preaching a kind of gradualism. Du Bois saw the black struggle for equality as part of a larger campaign for justice: "We want the laws enforced against rich as well as poor; against Capitalist as well as Laborer; against white as well as black," Du Bois wrote, and many agreed.

In 1913, in his first inaugural speech, President Woodrow Wilson looked back on the previous decade and scolded his fellow citizens for placing profit before loftier values. "With riches has come inexcusable waste," Wilson told them. "We have been proud of our industrial achievements, but we have not hitherto stopped thoughtfully enough to count the human cost."

Like Du Bois and Wilson, most of the great heroes of the early twentieth century were reformers. Progressivism, that great political tide that aimed to wash away graft and greed, had many champions. There were the muckrakers, pioneering investigative journalists such as Samuel Hopkins Adams, who alerted the public to the dangers of patent medicines; there were researchers such as Dr. Harvey W. Wiley, chief chemist for the U.S. Department of Agriculture, whose work led to the Pure Food and Drugs Act of 1906; and there were politicians such as "Fighting Bob" La Follette, a populist visionary who, upon getting elected governor of Wisconsin in 1900, spent the next 25 years campaigning for a series of farsighted measures to protect working people and make government more responsive to their needs.

But over this era when optimism warred with

self-criticism, there towered one man, Theodore Roosevelt, who served as president from Sept. 15, 1901 to March 4, 1909, when he was succeeded by his hand-picked candidate, William Howard Taft. A man of Roosevelt's great energy and optimism probably would have reached the White House one day, but Roosevelt got there faster than even he wished. On Sept. 6, 1901, second-term president William McKinley was shot while attending the Pan-American Exposition in Buffalo, by Leon Czolgosz, an anarchist. McKinley died eight days later, which made his 42-year-old vice president the youngest chief executive in U.S. history.

Though few men have had greatness thrust upon them so abruptly, Roosevelt was up to the task. His favorite word was "strenuous"—he was climbing in the Adirondacks when he received word of McKinley's assassination—and he strove to embody that adjective during the seven momentous years of his administration.

Roosevelt called his program the Square Deal, emphasizing the fairness he hoped to promote through his policies. "The great development of industrialism means that there must be an increase in the supervision exercised by the Government over the business enterprise," he said.

Believing that the "general welfare" clause of the Constitution gave him the power to act nationally, Roosevelt turned his ferocious energies on a host of business problems, busting up seemingly omnipotent oil and tobacco trusts, regulating railroads and pushing legislation on every subject that touched the ordinary worker, from workman's compensation to the eight-hour workday. Roosevelt successfully interceded in the great anthracite coal strike of 1902 and the following year persuaded Congress to create the Department of Commerce and Labor. Inspired by his love of the outdoors and by the work of the great conservationist John Muir, he

Muir (above) lobbied for conservation, a call heeded by the energetic Roosevelt (left).

set aside some 150 million acres of land as protected reserves.

Most men would have needed some rest by then. But Roosevelt, who had first come to prominence on foreign soil when he led the Rough Riders up San Juan Hill during the Spanish-American War, was almost as unwearying in the arena of foreign affairs. In 1903 he negotiated a treaty with Panama that led to the building of the Panama Canal and two years later mediated an end to the war between Japan and Russia, an act that won him the 1906 Nobel Prize for Peace and signaled the United States' move to the forefront of international affairs. Indeed, it is hard to imagine someone better equipped to lead the country into this complicated, fast-paced American century than the energetic Roosevelt.

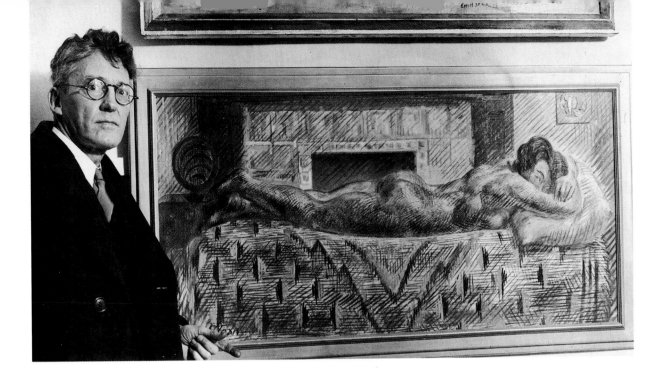

THE ASH CAN ARTISTS

The works of George Bellows, William Glackens, Robert Henri, George Luks, Everett Shinn and John Sloan—known collectively as the Ash Can Artists—revealed the energetic, chaotic and sometimes squalid character of New York City as it entered the twentieth century. Their probing depictions of teeming Lower East Side streets, harried dock workers and low-brow sometimes vulgar forms of entertainment shocked the art establishment by challenging the relevance and necessity of beauty in art. This radical departure from the genteel drawing-room and afternoon-in-the-park subject matter favored by the Impressionists earned them, at least initially, the status of pariahs or "refusés," as they were known within the art world.

Although the Ash Can Artists (1897-1917) were never a formal school—the openly derogatory sobriquet was applied to them by detractors in 1907—they met regularly, exchanged ideas and shared artistic beliefs. When Shinn, Glackens, Luks and Sloan first met Henri, the group's leader, at the Pennsylvania Academy of Fine Arts in the 1890s, they were working as sketch-reporters for Philadelphia's daily newspapers. Their experience in observing a scene, memorizing the telling details and churning out images under deadline pressure dovetailed with Henri's belief in working fast as a critical component in transmitting one's self onto the canvas. Between beer drinking and sketching at weekly studio openhouses, they listened to Henri expound on the importance of free thought, individualism, humanitarianism and democracy in art.

Ash Can Artists included Sloan (top) and Glackens, whose *Far from the Fresh Air Farm* (left) captured the tumult of urban life.

By 1904, Henri and his fellow Ash Can Artists had moved to New York in search of greater opportunity. Although most of them enjoyed recognition from published illustrations and cartoons, their breakthrough as painters came in 1907, when Henri resigned from the National Academy of Design's jury in protest over its stodginess—a move that grabbed the attention of an art press eager for scandal. With influential critics in their camp, the group put together an unprecedented independent exhibition called "The Eight," which included Maurice Prendergast, Ernest Lawson and Arthur B. Davies. (Bellows was not part of the show but was already making his reputation as a significant young talent.) The show, which went on to tour the United States, was highly publicized, received strong reviews and helped to free them from illustration as their primary means of support.

Also known as New York Realists, the Ash Can Artists were not the first painters to depict urban subjects—Manet and Degas, most notably, had portrayed city scenes some 50 years earlier. But the Ash Can Artists were unique in making the human experience of the city—as opposed to its architecture and design—the subject of their work. From street level they humanized the squalor of immigrant life, addressed the disparity between the wealthy and poor and illustrated the changing relations between men and women. In keeping with the spirit of poet Walt Whitman, an important influence, they celebrated the quotidian.

"When the Ash Can Artists depicted twentieth-century New York in its formative years, they captured early expressions of themes that still define the city today."
—ROBERT W. SNYDER, social and cultural historian, 1995

The Ash Can Artists depicted life as they found it on the street, as in Luks' *Bleecker and Carmine Streets* (opposite page), or in the illicit entertainments of the day, including boxing, as in Bellows' *Stag at Sharkey's* (above), and wrestling, as in Luks' *The Wrestlers* (left).

In spite of this shared approach, the Ash Can Artists' work was highly diverse. Sloan, the most politically engaged of the group, portrayed the upper class as vacuous while refraining from moral comment in his renderings of prostitutes. Glackens's animated street scenes, such as *Far from the Fresh Air Farm* (1911), captured the transformation of crowded Lower East Side neighborhoods under successive waves of immigration. With *Bleecker and Carmine Streets* (1905), Luks illustrated the lively sidewalk socializing of Italian immigrants in Greenwich Village. Shinn highlighted the raucous exchange between audience and performer in his depictions of vaudeville, and Henri conveyed the illicit thrill of female flesh in *Salome* (1909). Bellows, considered the most talented of the group, also focused on popular entertainment—such as boxing in his *Stag at Sharkey's* (1909)—but tackled larger subjects as well like the monumental human labor behind the city's rapid growth in a series on the excavation that preceded the construction of Pennsylvania Station.

When World War I stemmed the tide of immigration, and radicalism was replaced with fervent patriotism, the progressive spirit that motivated the Ash Can Artists became a thing of the past. By then, however, the group had altered the boundaries of acceptable art forever.

Bellows's vivid depiction (above) of the excavation for the construction of Pennsylvania Station attempted to capture the spirit of the actual site (left).

Aftermath

The notion of art as beauty, so effectively challenged by the Ash Can Artists, has all but disappeared in today's art world. Looking at the work of contemporary artists from Karen Findlay to Jeff Koons, one finds it hard to imagine any single person or movement having the same power to shock as the Ash Can Artists did in turn-of-the-century New York. Their influence extends from 1980s graffiti painter Keith Haring to a Seattle band which calls itself the Ashcan School.

THEODORE ROOSEVELT

A recently retired subway conductor in New York City was famous for announcing stations with a showman's flair while informing his passengers of the landmarks associated with each stop. The verve he brought to his work transformed a dreary trip into a flight of fancy, and invariably sent New Yorkers out the doors with smiles on their faces (no mean feat, that). As the train entered one station in particular he would often call out, "Now approaching 23rd Street. If you like Theodore Roosevelt, you may want to get out here. For this is where he got off."

Indeed Roosevelt did, to walk to his boyhood home on 20th Street. And Roosevelt would have deemed this trainman his kind of fellow: a person whose unstoppable enthusiasm and will could transform his surroundings. As Roosevelt once wrote, "I am only an average man but by George, I work harder at it than the average man."

While Roosevelt did work harder than the average man, he was hardly average. Said to have a photographic memory, he read two or three books a day. To call him energetic would be like calling a tornado gusty. He started writing his first book, on the War of 1812, as a student at Harvard, and would write 23 more, on subjects as varied as zoology, history, big-game hunting, politics and cattle ranching. His toughness bordered on the superhuman. In 1912, Roosevelt ran for president as a third-party candidate representing the Progressive, a.k.a. Bull Moose, Party. While campaigning in Milwaukee he was shot in the chest, but insisted on delivering his speech. He held up the bullet-pierced, blood-soaked manuscript for the stunned audience to see, saying, "It is true, I have just been shot. But it takes more than that to kill a bull moose." With blood darkening his shirt, he gave a shortened version of the speech before agreeing to get in an ambulance.

This hardiness, however, did not come naturally to Roosevelt. As a child he was frail and sickly, suffering from an array of ailments related to chronic

Roosevelt's vigorous speaking style (left) attracted large crowds (top) wherever he made a campaign stop.

"His personality so crowds the room that the walls are worn thin and threaten to burst outward."

—*AN UNKNOWN FRIEND*

asthma. "You have the mind but not the body," his father told him. "You must make your body." As the story goes, young Theodore gritted his teeth in the half grin, half growl that would become his trademark, and said, "I'll make my body. By heaven, I will."

And he did, molding himself into a barrel-chested, iron-willed adult who would not just live the strenuous life but attack it. He took his coffee with seven lumps of sugar in a cup his son Theodore Jr. said was "more in the nature of a bath-tub." He quit his comfortable post as assistant secretary of the navy to fight in the Spanish-American War, charging with his volunteer cavalry regiment, "Roosevelt's Rough Riders," up Cuba's San Juan Hill.

The tragedies of Roosevelt's life—and there were several, including the deaths on the same 1884 day of his mother and his first wife, Alice—did little to limit his boyish streak. Having been elected vice president in 1900, he ascended to the presidency when William McKinley was assassinated in 1901, then won the office on his own in 1904. Never before had an occupant of the White House romped

The young man at Harvard (far left) transformed himself into Roosevelt the Rough Rider (left), Roosevelt the doting father of six (near left) and Roosevelt the passionate believer in the value of protected wilderness (below, with a group of friends at the base of a giant redwood in Santa Cruz, California). His ebullience (far left, below) was, to put it mildly, infectious.

through its rooms on hands and knees, at play with his children. Roosevelt allowed his brood of six a menagerie of pets, including a badger, a macaw, several rabbits and a black bear. Pillow fights, with the chief executive in the fray, were a common occurrence. "You must always remember," a British diplomat once said, "that the president is about six."

But Roosevelt had no trouble drawing the line between work and play. He mediated labor disputes, curtailed trade monopolies, orchestrated the building of the Panama Canal and set aside more than 220 million acres of land for public use. In 1906 he won the Nobel Prize for Peace for brokering a settle-

"Speak softly and carry a big stick," was one of Roosevelt's oft-quoted aphorisms and, as the cartoon on the opposite page shows, he used that big stick to promote a variety of causes; ever the outdoorsman, Roosevelt loved riding, especially in his beloved Yellowstone Park (left); inspecting the fleet (opposite page), Roosevelt took his duties as commander-in-chief very seriously; Roosevelt's campaign paraphernalia included a button promoting racial equality (right, top).

ment to the yearlong border dispute between Russia and Japan in Manchuria. After his final run for the presidency in 1912, Roosevelt made an expedition to discover the source of a river in Brazil. He emerged with an infected leg, a high fever, and a river named in his honor—Rio Teodoro.

His image is also chiseled into the face of Mt. Rushmore, and appropriately so, for he embodied and indeed helped shape the American spirit. If he could have met the subway man who publicly remembered his childhood haunt, Roosevelt surely would have shaken his hand, complimented his style, and said, as he so often did, "Dee-lighted!"

Aftermath

Theodore Roosevelt's run for president on the Bull Moose ticket in 1912 split the Republican Party so severely that the election was essentially given to the Democratic candidate, Woodrow Wilson. Nonetheless, Roosevelt's achievement was substantial: He remains the only third-party candidate for president to get more votes than the candidate of one of the two established parties, having defeated Republican candidate William Howard Taft by nearly 700,000 votes.

ELLIS ISLAND

The distinguished roll call could fill a shelf of phone books: Irving Berlin (1893), Charles Atlas (1903), Bob Hope (1908), Claudette Colbert (1912), Rudolph Valentino and Elia Kazan (1913), Isaac Asimov (1923). On and on the names spin out, a veritable who's who of American achievement from every conceivable walk of life. All share one distinguishing characteristic: They began their lives in the United States as children wending their way through a maze of lines at Ellis Island, armed with little more than a small bundle of personal belongings and their family's hopes for a better existence.

Ellis Island has been rightly called the gateway to America. Just off the southern tip of Manhattan, this 3.5-acre parcel of land once used as a fishing base by Indians—and briefly owned by butcher Samuel Ellis—became the principal federal immigration station in the United States be-

tween 1892 and 1954. Of the 16 million immigrants who made their way to this country between 1892 and 1924, 12 million passed through the now hallowed historical site; on a single day in 1907, as many as 12,000 people landed there.

The immigrants, many of them from Eastern and Southern Europe, arrived by steamship, often after weeks on the turbulent open seas. Once in New York Harbor, passengers eager to disembark crowded the decks. To their right were the shores of Brooklyn, to their left, the raised arm of the Statue of Liberty, powerful symbol of their dream of a new life. For the wealthier first- and second-class passengers who had been processed on board, that new life could get under way immediately. But for the much more numerous poor, forced to spend most of their journey below deck in steerage, the ordeal was just beginning. Herded onto over-

Immigrants (left) arrived at Ellis Island (above) by the thousands, including 12,000 people on a single day in 1907.

crowded barges and ferries, they sometimes had to endure several days of anxious waiting before being shipped briefly back in the direction of Europe for the short trip to Ellis Island.

At the end of that trip there was yet more waiting, uncomfortable hours spent without food, water, or adequate toilets, before the new arrivals were allowed to set foot on American soil. Now the process quickened somewhat. Heavy bags were sometimes left on the ground floor and in some cases children were herded in one direction, adults in another. As the line of exhausted and fearful arrivals finally reached the imposing Great Hall on the second floor of the facility, U.S. Public Health Service doctors watched carefully for unsteady gaits, suspicious coughs or shortness of breath. Any hint of disease was noted with a swift scrawl in blue chalk on the shoulder of an immigrant's clothing: "L" for lameness, "H" for heart, "G" for goiter. About 10 percent of the immigrants were marked with an "X" for possible mental illness and detained for further questioning.

During the physical inspections, buttonhooks, hairpins or an inspector's own fingers were used to raise eyelids and check for signs of the blindness-inducing and highly contagious trachoma. Women, many of whom had never been touched by men other than their husbands, shuddered at the inspectors' foreign touch.

Legal inspectors grappled with (and allegedly quite often changed) tongue-twisting names such as Andrjuljawierjus and Zemiszkicivicz while rapid-firing a barrage of questions: Are you married or single? How much money do you have?

Arrivals (above) were marked by numbered cards (opposite page) that indicated the page and line numbers on which their names appeared on their ship's manifest.

"When we were getting off Ellis Island, we had all sorts of tags on us. Now that I think of it, we must have looked like marked-down merchandise at Gimbel's basement store...."

—*Anna Vida,*
Hungarian immigrant, 1921

Italians traveling in steerage (above) strained the capacity of their ship; the line of immigrants at Ellis Island began on the docks (left) and wended its way through the baggage room on the ground floor and up to the Great Hall on the second.

What is your occupation? Through the entire ordeal, the specter of deportation loomed large: the federal law that established the Bureau of Immigration in 1891 barred "persons likely to become public charges, idiots, insane persons, paupers, and polygamists." Two percent of immigrants did not pass their inspections.

The vast majority, of course, did. And today some 40 percent of all U.S. citizens can trace their ancestry to those whose first steps in America were taken on that tiny island hard by the glittering metropolis of New York. In that sense the children of Ellis Island are truly beyond number, its legacy renewed every day as yet another descendant draws first breath.

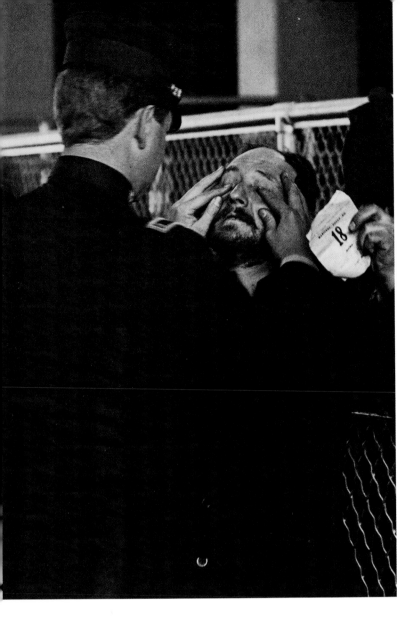

Aftermath

America's gateway was not to remain open forever. By the 1920s, with much more restrictive immigration laws in place, Ellis Island was primarily used for "assembly, detainment and deporting aliens." In 1954, Ellis Island was abandoned altogether, its 35 buildings left to rot until 1982, when the largest restoration project in U.S. history was undertaken to transform the former immigration station into a museum. Ellis Island reopened its doors in 1990 and now receives some two million visitors every year.

Families arrived with only what they were able to carry (above, left); the sometimes painful trachoma examinations (above) were among the least pleasant elements of the inspection process; meals at Ellis Island (left), featuring plain but wholesome fare, were multicultural events of the first order; after their long wait, a mother and daughter (right) sat in the now deserted Great Hall.

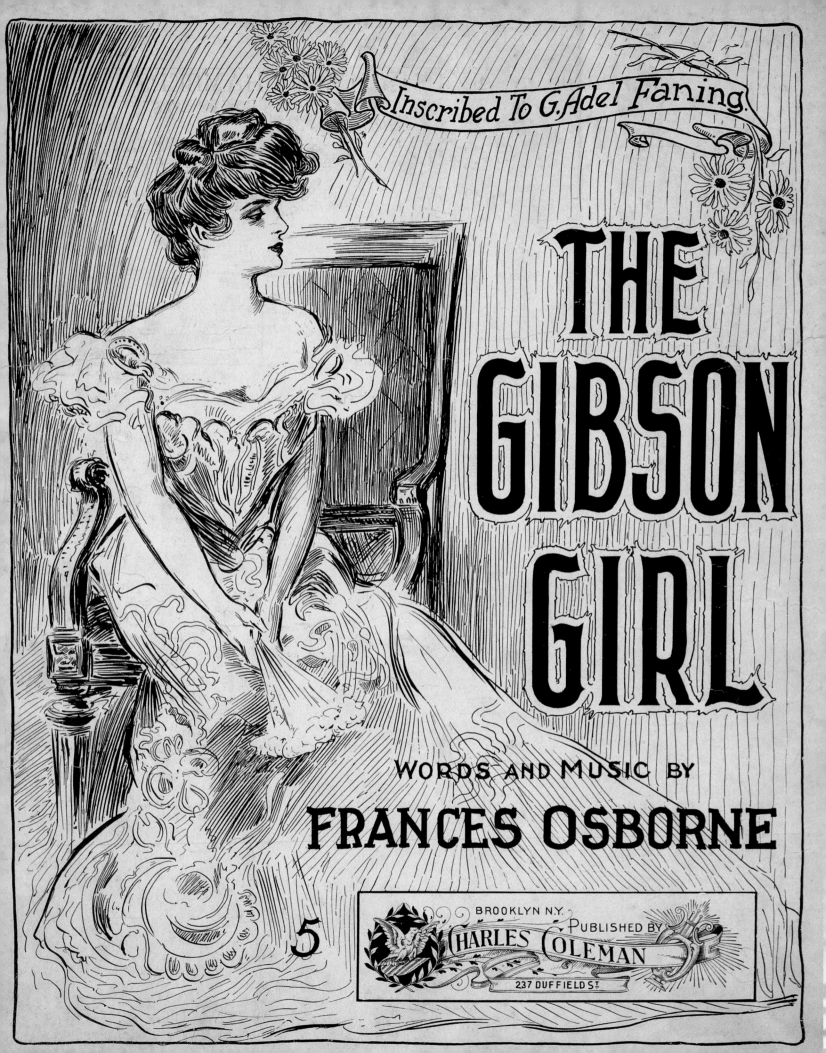

THE GIBSON GIRL

At the height of her popularity, the Gibson girl was everywhere: on ashtrays, umbrella stands, dresser sets and whisk-broom holders. In homes around the country, Gibson albums lay atop parlor tables, while large-scale reproductions of her lithesome figure graced the walls. A favored hobby had thousands scorching Gibson images onto miles of leather strips and wooden panels. There was even a wallpaper designed for bachelors' bedrooms, depicting the many serene and self-assured visages of the Gibson girl.

Created by social satirist and illustrator Charles Dana Gibson, the Gibson girl, singular, was actually a composite of the many vibrant and beautiful young women drawn by Gibson that first appeared in the late 1800s as pen-and-ink drawings on the pages of the weekly humor magazine *Life*, as well as in other popular publications like *Collier's*, *Harper's* and *Scribners*. By 1900, Gibson's serialized picture stories had readers practically ripping through *Life*, partly for the quick wit Gibson employed to poke fun at society foibles, but mostly to absorb the style, beauty and elegance of the Gibson girl.

Part college girl, part fashion beauty, she could buy a hat from the finest milliner in London one day, and wear a sensible, utilitarian skirt and neat white blouse to her office job the next. Her hair was fixed in a pompadour, her handshake was firm, and she strode with a sense of confidence and new-found emancipation from the nineteenth century into the twentieth, always with a trail of handsome men—ideally with the so-called Gibson man among them—behind her.

To a rapidly expanding middle class, the Gibson girl embodied the independent spirit of the "new woman." The nation's five million working women—many now supporting themselves as typists, thanks to the recent birth of the Reming-

The success of the Gibson girl (top) spawned a host of products, including popular songs such as the one at left.

ton—drew from the fashion template she provided to bring a look of dignity and efficiency to their jobs. "You can always tell when a girl is taking the Gibson cure," remarked one contemporary observer, "by the way she fixes her hair." To say nothing of the way her large bosom perched over a tiny, pinched waist. Thanks to mail order, the so-called Gibson look was available to any woman who could get her hands on a Sears Roebuck catalogue. The Gibson-inspired shirtwaist alone was offered by the company in 150 varieties, featuring straight or leg-of-mutton sleeves, collars that stood up or turned down, and necks that came ruffled or studded with small black ties. When a bustle, corset, flounced skirt and jaunty hat were added to the shirtwaist—voilà—one had all the makings of the Gibson "office look."

"I'm only a bird in a gilded cage, a beautiful sight to see," went the lyrics of a popular song. And although by current standards the constraining devices demanded by the Gibson look—with its sought-after S-shaped curve—could not have been comfortable, they were still a marked improvement over the well-ribbed, heavy steel corsetry of bygone days. Simpler, more sensible fashion had broken through and sporty women of the new era had reason to celebrate.

Before Gibson synthesized his ideal woman, the American girl was vague, nondescript, inchoate. As soon as the world saw Gibson's ideal, it bowed down in adoration, saying: "Lo, at last the typical American girl."
—The New York *World*

With the help of the Sears Roebuck catalogue, any woman could create the Gibson look (left).

The nation's fascination with all things Gibson transcended even the world of fashion, inspiring several songs, including *Why Do They Call Me the Gibson Girl?* (from the 1906 musical *The Belle of Mayfair*), as well as a revue, *The Gibson Bathing Girl*, that was performed by the Ziegfeld Follies in 1907.

As insightful as Gibson's portraits of a self-assured upper class and an aspiring middle class were, he himself was born, in 1867, into a family of humble means. As a boy he passed up pens and brushes in favor of scissors, exhibiting extraordinary talent for lively, detailed silhouettes of birds, fish and people. In 1886, following two years at New York's Art Students League and a rocky start as an illustrator, Gibson managed to sell a small and relatively crude drawing to *Life*. It netted him four dollars.

That of course was a pittance in comparison to the income Gibson would later earn, once his liberal licensing policy had established the Gibson girl as a full-blown craze. Of course, crazes that wax hot must eventually cool, and Gibson's was no exception. In this case, however, the impact of his work would outlive the drawings themselves as women strode more and more confidently into the new century.

Gibson's moment in the sun was brief, but the impact of his drawings would be felt long after the craze had passed.

Aftermath

America's passion for the Gibson girl diminished in the wake of World War I as Gibson's untroubled takes on society life no longer jibed with the nation's more complicated, less confident view of itself. Although Gibson carried on—continuing to illustrate, and for a time editing *Life*—the world of the Gibson girl had vanished forever.

THE GREAT TRAIN ROBBERY

In the 102 years that have passed since the first program of short films was presented in Paris on December 28, 1895, few filmmakers have beguiled their audiences as skillfully as Edwin S. Porter did in the final scene of his groundbreaking 1903 film, *The Great Train Robbery*. In it, a scowling gunslinger draws his pistol and fires two shots directly into the camera before vanishing in a cloud of gunsmoke. So totally unexpected was the act, so new the medium, that panic-stricken audiences fled from theaters.

As arresting as that moment is, the greatness of *The Great Train Robbery* rests on more subtle tricks. Just 10 minutes long, with a rather conventional plot of crime, pursuit and punishment, *The Great Train Robbery* contains a virtual encyclopedia of cinematic techniques that would come to be part of the basic language of film. Many film scholars consider it the first "real" movie.

By placing his camera right in the middle of the action, Porter placed his audience there, too. In one scene the camera was situated on top of the moving train, so that the robbers climbing up the side would make their entrance from the bottom of the frame. Porter also cut between scenes without dissolves or fades, to give the impression of events transpiring simultaneously, and he used panning shots to heighten the sense of speed and movement.

Porter even created primitive special effects, using skillful stop-motion photography to film actors throwing dummies off the train. At the time the early French director Georges Méliès was also using visual tricks, but his were not an integral part of the action, and they tended to feel like set pieces. Most significant of all, Porter understood intuitively that the frame, rather than the scene, was the basic unit of film. Thus, through imaginative editing, he was able to cre-

The final gunshot fired directly into the camera (left) sent moviegoers fleeing from theaters like the one above.

The film, which included violent sequences such as the one above and at right, depicted a daring train robbery (top) and escape (opposite page); the movie's success helped establish the Western as a staple of American filmmaking.

34

"Porter's shrewdly edited images advanced the narrative frame by frame, generating an excitement that no movie before it had approached."

—*TED SENETT, film historian, 1990*

ate a movie that sped along more suspensefully than any of its predecessors.

Porter did not set out to make film history. Born in Connellsville, Pennsylvania, on April 21, 1870, he spent his first years in the nascent film industry as a projectionist and mechanic. In partnership with William Beadnell, he invented the Beadnell "improved projector." But when fire gutted the company's warehouse in 1900, Porter had to find other work. After a stint as a free-

lance photographer, he joined the Thomas A. Edison Company and soon climbed to the position of film production chief. In 1902 Porter made his first serious film, *Life of an American Fireman.*

Edison did not agree with some of Porter's ideas, such as showing just parts of actors. Edison argued that the camera ought to show a person in his entirety. In 1909 their disagreements drove Porter to form his own company, Rex Films. When it was sold in 1912, the most important di-

Thomas Edison, an early employer of Porter (right), invented one of the first "moving picture machines" (far right), which helped pave the way for the five-cent theaters (left) and solidify the movies as America's most popular art form.

rector of film's first decade was forced to the sidelines. A rare visionary with technical skills to match, Porter continued to experiment with color technology, synchronized sound and 3-D film until his death 1941.

Along with its technical achievements, *The Great Train Robbery* was tremendously important for the movie business in a purely economic sense. It was the first of many successful Westerns—though it was shot in New Jersey—and its great popularity propelled the new medium into the public's consciousness at a time when the novelty of moving pictures was beginning to wear off. Just as years later, at the start of the "talkie" era, virtually every new theater opened with Al Jolson's *The Jazz Singer*, so in the years following 1903 did every Nickelodeon that opened around the country seem to show *The Great Train Robbery*.

And open they did. Porter and his fellow directors had to scramble to keep up with the demand for new films. In 1905 Porter spoofed his first great success with *The Little Train Robbery*, in which a gang of children hold up a toy train and are caught by policemen in rowboats. In 1908 Porter's artistic heir, D.W. Griffith, made three Westerns in his first month at Biograph Studios. He went on to make countless others, all of which now look like preparation for *Birth of a Nation* (1915), America's first great movie epic.

Aftermath

Westerns have continued to do well in Hollywood. When Clint Eastwood's dark *Unforgiven* won the 1992 Academy Award for Best Picture, it was the third time a Western had earned the film world's grandest prize—the other winners were *Cimarron* (1931) and *Dances with Wolves* (1990). Other classics of the genre include *High Noon* (1952) and *Shane* (1953).

MODEL T

A wooden-wheeled vehicle that, in a bind, could run on a brew of kerosene and candlestick ends would seem an unlikely source of revolution. But Henry Ford's Model T was the driving force behind an industry that thoroughly altered the social and economic profile of the United States in just two decades.

When introducing the first Model T in 1908 with the words "I will build a car for the great multitude," Ford spoke not as a sociologist or as a politician, but as a self-taught engineer and perennial tinkerer. In fact, Ford, who was raised on a farm in Dearborn, Michigan, would later express his dismay at the rural exodus made possible by his Tin Lizzie, or flivver, as the inexpensive Model T came to be affectionately called.

Until the first Model T rolled off the assembly line in 1908, automobiles sold for upward of $5,000 and thus were reserved for the wealthy. Thanks to his groundbreaking system of mass production, Ford was able to price the first Tin Lizzie at a mere $850. As the years passed, further improvements to assembly line techniques led to even greater economies of scale and ultimately lower prices. "Every time I lower the price a dollar, we gain a thousand new buyers," Ford declared in 1916, revealing a sales philosophy that his competitors found truly incomprehensible. By 1916 the Model T cost only $360 and was well within the reach of the common man. In 1914, a minimum wage hike to $5 a day enabled even Ford's factory workers to purchase their company's most popular product.

It is impossible to overstate the significance of the changes wrought by Ford's affordable cars. Farms were now just an afternoon's drive from urban centers. Acreage formerly planted with hay to feed horses was freed up for cash crops. Cities spread, suburbs sprang up, and a network of highways crisscrossed the country. Almost

Ford (left) and his earth-shattering invention quickly became familiar fixtures on the American scene.

"The jokes about my car sure helped to popularize it. I hope they never end."
—*HENRY FORD*

The love affair between the Model T and its owners (below) was based on its cheap price, as stated in an ad for the first model (far right), as well as its versatility—the flivver could serve as a farm vehicle (above) or a family getaway car (right); in whatever guise, it spelled the end of the horse (opposite page, below) as a primary means of transportation.

overnight, the automobile had become a pillar of the American economy. In 1914 alone, 240,700 Model T's were manufactured, almost as many as all other makes of cars combined. By the end of the twentieth century's second decade, nearly four million Model T's were on the road and the Tin Lizzie had become an accepted part of the American lexicon, even generating a wealth of jokes based on its inexpensive components. "I hear they are going to magnetize the rear axle of the Ford," began one such bit.

"What's the idea?"

"So it will pick up the parts that drop off."

Rattles, bumpy rides and a somewhat ungainly profile aside, the four-cylinder, 20-horsepower Model T was so simple by design that any handy person with basic tools could fix it. Replacement parts such as mufflers and new fenders cost 25 cents and $2.50 respectively. Some owners even argued that fenders that softened and wrinkled made it easier to get in and out of tight spots.

Whether in the guise of a roadster, a coupe, a delivery truck or one of its other half-dozen variations, the flivver ran roughshod over other motorized vehicles. As one anecdote attested, the Model T

could go just about anywhere: A dying man had a final request—that his flivver be buried with him, for as he put it, he had never been in a hole that his Ford didn't get him out of. With special attachments, she could even pump water, plow fields and generate electricity.

Although various changes were made to the Model T over the years—the headlights went from acetylene to electric, the body from wood to metal, the wheels from wood to integrally welded spoke steel—the engine, transmission and chassis remained unaltered. Even the color, black, remained the same. It is hardly surprising, then, that by 1927 the Model T had fallen behind the times and production ceased.

In 19 years, 15.5 million Model T's had sold in the United States, and another 1.25 million in Canada and Great Britain, equaling half of the world's automobile production. The tinkerer had changed the very face of America.

Ford's means of production may seem crude today, but they represented the beginnings of the modern assembly line—the Model T's flywheel magneto (far left) was the first manufactured part to be built on a moving assembly line; the early Tin Lizzies were built on a so-called "push" assembly line (above, left), while the final assembly line (above) called for the Ford body to be skidded down a wooden ramp and onto the waiting chassis.

Aftermath

The Model T was not, of course, the only car that Henry Ford's company produced. The corporation he created remains one of the world's leading automobile manufacturers today, its worldwide sales surpassed only by General Motors. In the tradition of the Model T, Ford continues to lead the way in the creation and marketing of affordable vehicles: The Ford Escort has been the top-selling small car in the United States every year since it was introduced in 1982.

JOHN MUIR

"When I was a boy in Scotland I was fond of everything that was wild, and all my life I've been growing fonder and fonder of wild places and wild creatures," wrote John Muir at the beginning of *The Story of My Boyhood and Youth.* If it is possible for a single sentence to sum up as rich and remarkable a life as Muir's, that one does it. Muir loved nature as few men ever have, with a passion that was deeply spiritual. He was a natural philosopher, an explorer, an inventor and a talented writer, blessed with a poet's gift for communicating all of his enthusiasm. Read today, essays such as "The Mountains of California," and "Stickeen," his account of a trek through Alaska in the company of a small wonderful dog, seem as fresh and clear as the "ice-streams" he describes in "Yosemite Glaciers."

Today we remember Muir as the father of America's conservation movement. He did more to preserve the American wilderness than anyone else. Congress didn't create the National Park Service until 1916, two years after his death, but Muir was the driving force behind the establishment of Yosemite, Mt. Rainier, the Petrified Forest and the Grand Canyon as national parks.

Muir was born on April 21, 1838, in Dunbar, a small town on Scotland's rugged east coast, where his father, Daniel, was a grocer whose prosperousness was exceeded only by his piousness. A strict Christian fundamentalist, Daniel Muir was a harsh disciplinarian, and one wonders whether the raptures John Muir experienced in the immensity of the American West owed their intensity to the strictures of his boyhood.

Muir (left), an ardent lover of wild places and wild creatures, worked tirelessly to preserve natural sites such as Mt. Rainier (top).

When Muir was 11, his father shocked him by announcing that the family was to sail for America the next day. Upon at last reaching their new home in the forests of Wisconsin, Muir and his younger brother, David, raced around like happy kittens, looking for birds' nests and marveling at meadows full of lightning bugs. "This sudden splash into pure wildness—baptism in Nature's warm heart—how utterly happy it made us!" he later recalled.

Muir spent several years at the University of Wisconsin but left before getting his degree to indulge a young man's dream of wandering the world. In 1867, while working at a carriage shop in Indianapolis, he slipped and drove a file into his right eye, blinding it. His left eye soon developed a sympathetic blindness. Though he regained his sight in both eyes over the next several months, he took the accident as a sign that he should begin his life's work of exploring the natural world. He walked 1,000 miles from Louisville, Kentucky, to the Gulf of Mexico; he sailed to Cuba and later to Panama, crossing the Isthmus and sailing up the West Coast to San Francisco. Though he would remain an incorrigible tramp for the rest of his life, traveling to South America and Africa at the age of 73, Muir found a home in northern California. He married Louie Strentzel in 1880 and they raised two children on her family's fruit ranch in Martinez.

In 1869 Muir spent his first summer in the Sierra working as a shepherd, and nothing in the world would ever stir him like the sight of his beloved California mountains. Standing on the summit of Pacheco Pass, with the Great Central Valley spread out to the west, he was in paradise: " … from the eastern boundary of this vast golden flower-bed rose the mighty Sierra, miles in height, and so gloriously colored and so radiant, it

"**Everybody needs beauty as well as bread, places to play in and pray in, where nature may heal and give strength to body and soul alike."**

—*JOHN MUIR, 1911*

Muir's elegant prose persuaded millions of Americans, such as the women at Yosemite on the opposite page, to visit wilderness areas, including Yellowstone (left), which gained federal protection in large measure due to Muir's initiative.

seemed not clothed with light but wholly composed of it, like the wall of some celestial city."

In 1892 Muir and his supporters founded the Sierra Club "to do," in Muir's words, "something for wildness and make the mountains glad." He was anxious to protect the forests, which were coveted by stockmen, and for years he stymied a plan to dam Yosemite's Hetch Hetchy Valley. His fame as a conservationist spread, and in 1903

President Theodore Roosevelt visited him in Yosemite, where the pair hiked and laid the foundation for Roosevelt's conservation initiatives.

Muir died of pneumonia on December 24, 1914. Though 75 years later his birthday was officially made John Muir Day in California, the most fitting monuments to his life were always the forests, glaciers, flowers and animals of his beloved mountains.

Muir (below, with conservation ally Theodore Roosevelt) traveled the world but always returned to California, where he helped foster a sense of awe about the wilderness, and especially about such natural wonders as the Cathedral Rocks (right) and towering forests (left) of Yosemite.

Aftermath

Since its founding in 1892 with John Muir as its first president, the Sierra Club has grown into conservation's most steadfast champion, working to preserve our natural heritage in part through the establishment and expansion of the system of national parks so valued by Americans today. The club has 550,000 members and conducts more than 350 nature outings annually.

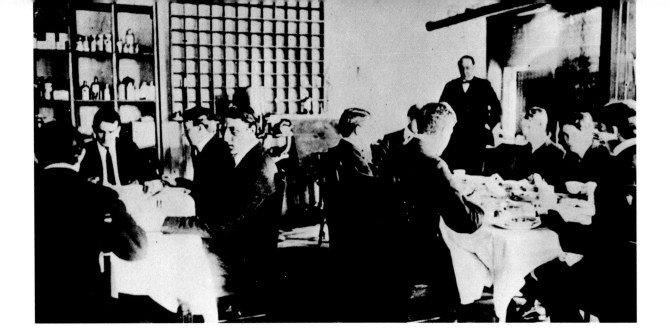

Pure Food and Drugs Act

The Progressive movement of the late nineteenth century found the perfect champion in Dr. Harvey Washington Wiley. A giant of a man with untameable hair and a disarming wit, Wiley had grown up in an evangelical Indiana home, and he brought to his lifelong crusade for safer food a zealot's fervor. As chief chemist for the U.S. Department of Agriculture from 1883 to 1912, Wiley made many contributions to public health and safety: He set up "poison squads"—teams of well-trained chemists that crisscrossed the country conducting ambush tests on food wherever it was distributed or eaten—and later established the Good Housekeeping Seal of Approval. But Wiley's greatest triumph was the Pure Food and Drugs Act, a watershed bill that created the Food and Drug Administration, gave it unprecedented power to regulate the content of food and drugs, and required warning labels on all habit-forming medications. A grateful public showed its appreciation for Wiley's efforts by referring to the bill as Dr. Wiley's Law.

Until Dr. Wiley and his followers came along, chicanery and lies ruled the free market, and every citizen had to be his own watchdog. "Study the medicine advertising in your morning paper," advised the great muckraking journalist Samuel Hopkins Adams, "and you will find yourself in a veritable goblin-realm of fakery, peopled with monstrous myths."

In the almost total absence of scientific testing and published standards, though, caveat emptor was cruel advice. Even reputable magazines such as *Harper's* carried ads for patent medicines promising quick cures for everything from cancer and cholera to diabetes, bad backs and opium addiction. One itinerant quack actually promised to restore sight to the blind by removing their eyeballs, scraping

Wiley's poison squad (top) searched for tainted food; another target was the overblown claims of patent medicines (left).

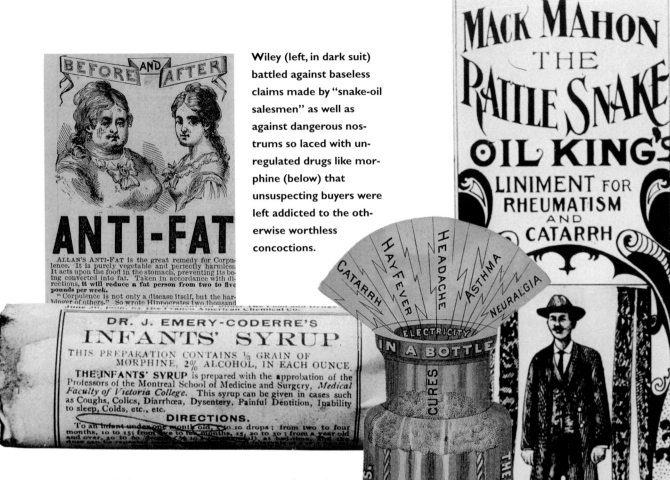

the backs of them and then reinserting them in their sockets.

Drug addiction was a national epidemic. Two to five percent of all American adults were addicts. Some were Civil War veterans, so many of whom were still addicted to morphine that the condition was commonly known as "soldiers' disease." But countless others were ordinary citizens who, having begun to take one of the myriad of opium-laced nostrums, quickly found themselves powerless to stop.

Wiley was, of course, a powerful force for change inside the government. Agitating on the outside were the so-called "muckrakers," a generation of idealistic journalists who called the public's attention to the many frauds committed against it. Under the editorship of William Allen White, the *Emporia Gazette* led the way by publicizing the hazards of self-medication with patent medicines. Edward Bok, the public-service-minded

> **"[The patent medicine industry] is a shameful trade that stupefies helpless babies and makes criminals of our young men and harlots of our young women."**
> —*SAMUEL HOPKINS ADAMS, 1905*

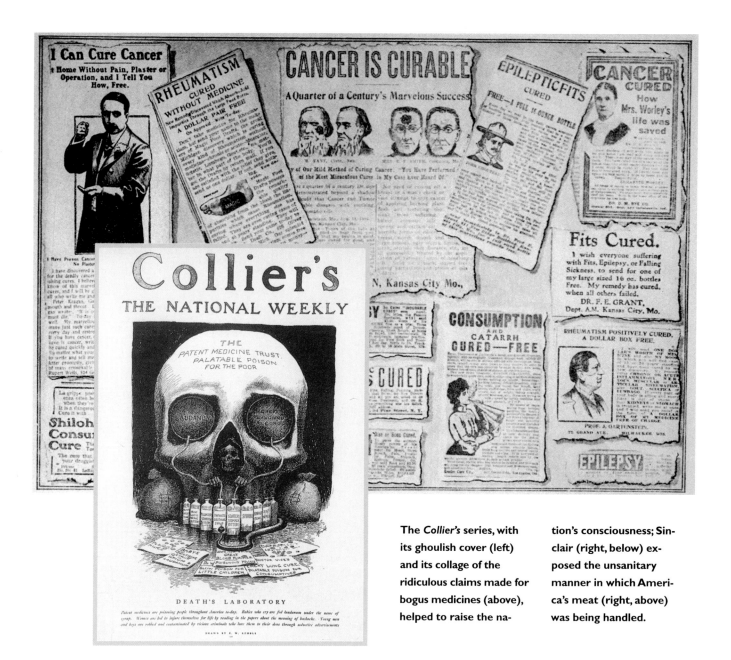

DEATH'S LABORATORY

The *Collier's* series, with its ghoulish cover (left) and its collage of the ridiculous claims made for bogus medicines (above), helped to raise the nation's consciousness; Sinclair (right, below) exposed the unsanitary manner in which America's meat (right, above) was being handled.

editor of the *Ladies Home Journal*, preached against pharmaceutical quackery and put principle above profit in 1892 by refusing to accept advertising for patent medicines. But the most important piece of muckraking journalism was probably Adams's "The Great American Fraud" series, which began appearing in *Collier's* in 1905. In it, Adams slammed the patent medicine industry as "a shameful trade that stupefies helpless babies and makes criminals of our young men and harlots of our young women."

Most famous of all muckraking novels was *The Jungle*, Upton Sinclair's bestselling exposé of the Chicago meatpacking industry. Published in 1906, it is the story of Jurgis Rudkus, a trusting Lithuanian immigrant who finds work in the stockyards before corruption and disregard for safety turn his dream into nightmare. Basing the novel on research funded by the Socialist party, Sinclair aimed to win sympathy for "wage slaves" in unregulated industries. Instead, he shocked the public with his gruesome descriptions of food preparation. "I aimed at the public's heart," said Sinclair, "and I hit it in the stomach."

By the time President Theodore Roosevelt signed the Pure Food and Drugs Act on June 30, 1906, Sinclair and the muckrakers had done their job, creating a groundswell of outrage over unsafe food and drugs. Though debate over government regulation continues today, few can question the importance of Wiley's historic victory.

Aftermath

With the Pure Food and Drugs Act, Congress established the principle of government oversight in key areas of public health and safety. That oversight was broadened by the Harrison Tax Act of 1914, which stringently regulated cocaine and heroin, and the Food, Drug and Cosmetic Act of 1938, which greatly extended the range of commodities under government control and stiffened the penalties for circumventing the law.

CRAYOLA CRAYONS

From an artistic point of view, 1903 was a very good year for children in America. After all, it gave rise to three instant classics: Kate Douglas Wiggin's *Rebecca of Sunnybrook Farm*, Jack London's *The Call of the Wild* and last, but far from least, Crayola crayons.

Until Crayolas were invented, crayons came in only a few colors and were limited to industrial use as markers. So when Crayolas hit the market at a nickel per box of eight no-nonsense colors (black, brown, orange, purple, yellow, red and green), kids went crazy for them.

Who put crayons in the hands of America's kids? Edwin Binney and Harold Smith, two Easton, Pennsylvania, industrialists who had already made their mark on the landscape by creating the red oxide pigments that became ubiquitous on this country's barns in the 1800s. In 1912 Binney and Smith helped turn automobile tires from white, and not particularly durable, to black and five times stronger, by convincing the Goodrich company to add carbon black pigments to its wares.

While Binney and Smith were touring Pennsylvania schools in 1903 to spread the word about their latest inventions—slate pencils and so-called An-Du-Septic dustless chalk (the latter would win a gold medal for technical innovation at the 1904 World's Fair in St. Louis)—they realized the students needed a little more color in their lives. Soon Binney and Smith began adapting their industrial crayons, adding color pigments to paraffin wax and pouring it into smaller molds, to fit little hands.

The name Crayola comes from "craie," French for "chalk," and "oleaginous," English for oily, and it has indeed stuck to the American consciousness like so much oily chalk. The Binney & Smith company reports that the average North American goes through 730 crayons by

The shift from white chalk to glorious color (left) was a cause for celebration among America's children (top).

Fuchsia

The sunset color
That summer twilight paints on
The brick facade, as
I sit on my porch watching
Elm shadows creep up the wall.

—*DOUG TANOURY,*
from "Crayola Poems," 1997

the age of 10, and that kids between the ages of two and eight average almost 30 minutes per day of coloring. Crayolas' appeal reaches farther than mere artistry, however. In a study of U.S. adults conducted by Yale University, the smell of Crayola crayons ranked 18th among the 20 most recognized odors in the world. That last statistic should come as no surprise: Crayolas are now labeled in 11 languages and sold in 60 countries, and the 100 billion crayons Binney & Smith has manufactured since 1903 would circle the globe four-and-a-half times if placed end to end.

The original eight-color selection has blossomed over the years: In 1949, it grew to 48 colors; in 1958, to 64, with a sharpener built into the box, no less. The most recent expansion came in 1993, when Crayola released its Big Box of 96 colors.

Over the years, color and name changes have been made to keep up with the times. In 1949, when teachers informed Binney & Smith that children no longer understood the term Prussian, the company changed Prussian Blue to Midnight Blue. In 1962, in the midst of the civil rights era, Flesh got a new name, Peach. Ten years later, in a nod to the mod, eight fluorescent colors were added to the mix.

Controversy abounded in 1990, when Binney

The original Binney & Smith plant along the Bushkill Creek in Easton, Pennsylvania manufactured a variety of products, including (clockwise, from top, opposite page) the prize-winning An-Du-Septic dustless crayons, the Rubens artists' Crayola, the colored chalk crayons and, of course, the children's Crayola.

& Smith retired eight colors. Blue Gray, Green Blue, Lemon Yellow, Maize, Orange Red, Orange Yellow, Raw Umber and Violet Blue gave way to Cerulean, Dandelion, Fuchsia, Jungle Green, Royal Purple, Teal Blue, Vivid Tangerine and Wild Strawberry. The National Campaign to Save Lemon Yellow and RUMPS—the Raw Umber and Maize Preservation Society— lost their battles. Fred Rogers must have been disappointed: Lemon Yellow had long been the favorite in "Mr. Rogers' Neighborhood."

Surely he has found a new favorite among the 96 Crayola offerings. With names culled from the suggestions of nearly two million consumers, the colors include Asparagus, Denim, Macaroni and Cheese, Purple Mountains Majesty, Tickle Me Pink and Tropical Rainforest.

One can only imagine what colors await us in the next millennium.

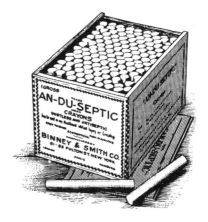

Aftermath

Crayola now produces some two billion crayons annually, at an average of five million crayons per day. North American children spend 6.3 billion hours coloring every year, the equivalent of 10,000 lifetimes. The two favorite colors used by children are, as they have no doubt been from the beginning, red and blue.

W.E.B. Du Bois

Born in Great Barrington, Massachusetts, in 1868, just five years after the Emancipation Proclamation was signed, W.E.B. Du Bois became a leading force in the struggle to secure full and equal citizenship for African-Americans in the first half of the twentieth century.

A sociologist, essayist, activist, and the first African-American to receive a Ph.D. from Harvard University (in 1895), Du Bois (pronounced Doo Boys) was often referred to as the dean of Negro intellectuals. From his platform as a teacher and social researcher at Atlanta University at the end of the nineteenth century, he proclaimed: "Race antagonism can only be stopped by intelligence." His belief that college-educated blacks should lead the fight against racism placed him squarely in opposition to Booker T. Washington, the most prominent African-American figure of the time, who thought blacks should develop technical and mechanical skills above all else.

Du Bois was a somewhat reluctant recruit to activism. In his second autobiography he wrote, "In 1905 I was still a teacher at Atlanta University and was in my imagination a scientist, and neither a leader nor an agitator." Yet he felt "one could not be a calm, cool, and detached scientist while Negroes were lynched, murdered and starved."

That same year Du Bois formed the Niagara Movement, whose resolution stated: "We claim for ourselves every single right that belongs to a freeborn American, political, civil, and social; and until we get these rights we will never cease to protest and assail the ears of America." Niagara, however, was hampered by limited funds and a membership confined to blacks.

On February 12, 1909—the 100th anniversary of Abraham Lincoln's birthday—60 intellectuals, philanthropists, social workers and African-American activists issued a call to create an orga-

As the NAACP's director of publications, Du Bois, with his staff (top), helped to define the debate on race in America.

nization that would fight for racial equality. The National Association for the Advancement of Colored People was born. Du Bois left Atlanta for New York to become a founding member of the Association, whose platform was virtually identical to Niagara's.

In its first 14 years the NAACP won groundbreaking court victories against taxation without representation (1910), residential segregation (1917), and, in 1923, the exclusion of blacks from juries. During those heady early days and until 1934, Du Bois was the NAACP's director of publications and research. In that role he edited a monthly magazine, *The Crisis*, in which he spoke out against the social, educational and political issues that beleaguered the African-American community. A philosophical split—Du Bois supported the idea of "purposeful segregation" which the NAACP did not condone—led him to resign and return to Atlanta in 1934. That split was echoed

"I believe in liberty for all men; the space to stretch their arms and souls; the right to breathe and the right to vote, the freedom to choose their friends, enjoy the sunshine and ride on the railroads...."

—*W.E.B. DU BOIS, 1905*

in the '60s in the faultline dividing Malcolm X and Martin Luther King Jr., and it persists to this day between those favoring various forms of black separatism and those of a more integrationist mindset. Du Bois rejoined the NAACP from 1944 to 1948, but grew increasingly frustrated by the slow progress it was making in its fight to improve race relations.

Informed in part by extensive travels throughout the world, Du Bois came to locate the roots of class and racial inequality in the exploitive nature of capitalism and its systems of colonization. He was impressed by the social experiments he witnessed in the Soviet Union and China and sought support in those countries for his idea of Pan-Africanism, or solidarity of the world's darker peoples. These views led him inevitably to a flirtation with communism, which he saw as "a planned way of life in the production of wealth and work designed for building a state whose object is the highest welfare of its people." This shift to the left, along with his participation in the Peace Information Center—an organization viewed by those infected with the anti-communist hysteria of the day as a Marxist front—led the federal government to refuse him the right to travel abroad from 1952 to 1957 and made him a controversial figure even among his fellow civil rights activists.

Du Bois spent his last two years in Ghana. When he died in 1963 at the age of 95, he left behind 18 books on sociology, history, politics and race relations, two autobiographies, several works of fiction, and a stunning, if at times contradictory, collection of ideas that altered forever the discourse about race relations in the United States and beyond.

THE CRISIS

A RECORD OF THE DARKER RACES

Volume One   NOVEMBER, 1910   Number One

Edited by W. E. BURGHARDT DU BOIS, with the co-operation of Oswald Garrison Villard,
J. Max Barber, Charles Edward Russell, Kelly Miller, W. S. Braithwaite and M. D. Maclean.

CONTENTS

Along the Color Line   3
Opinion   7
Editorial   10
The N. A. A. C. P.   12
Athens and Browns-
    ville   13
        By MOORFIELD STOREY
The Burden   14
What to Read . . .   15

PUBLISHED MONTHLY BY THE
National Association for the Advancement of Colored People
AT TWENTY VESEY STREET   NEW YORK CITY

ONE DOLLAR A YEAR   TEN CENTS A COPY

In 1917, during his years at the **NAACP**, **Du Bois** participated in an anti-lynching march (second row, second from right) as well as writing and editing *The Crisis*, the **NAACP's** journal devoted to the struggle for equality.

Aftermath

Almost 40 years after his state burial in Ghana, Du Bois continues to inspire generations of activists, scholars and politicians. The nation's oldest research center for black studies, the W.E.B. Du Bois Institute for Afro-American Research, bears the Promethean leader's name. Victories that Du Bois and the NAACP achieved in court are now written into law: The Civil Rights Act (1957, 1960 and 1964), the Voting Rights Act of 1965, the Fair Housing Act of 1968. But much remains to be done. Du Bois proclaimed some 100 years ago that racial division would be the greatest problem of the twentieth century, and indeed it remains one of the toughest challenges we face as a nation.

KITTY HAWK

A fateful coin toss landed Orville Wright, and not his brother Wilbur, in the pilot's position of the 1903 Flyer on the cold, windy morning of December 17, 1903. As he slid into the cradle of the 605-pound flying machine, any concerns about the strong winds and icy grounds at Kitty Hawk, N.C., were calmed by his cool confidence that years of scrupulous calculations and rigorous testing would at last send the Wright Brothers' flying machine gloriously airborne.

With the engine sufficiently warmed up, Orville gently released the machine from its starting track. Wilbur ran alongside, keeping the wings in balance as the flying machine shot forward on the track. When it reached the end of the track, Wilbur let go and watched in awe. The small crowd of witnesses erupted in cheers. The 1903 Flyer lifted off into the 27 mile-per-hour headwind for a 12-second flight covering 120 feet. Orville and Wilbur Wright became the first men in history to produce a self-powered aircraft capable of sustaining independent flight.

Innately curious, creative and mechanically inclined, the Wright Brothers achieved their success despite having little education and not much money. As young adults in their hometown of Dayton, Ohio, they built a printing press that could print a thousand pages an hour. Years later their printing business put out a weekly paper called the *West Side News*, which they eventually converted into a daily, *The Evening Item*.

Capitalizing on the bicycle craze that was sweeping the nation in the early 1890s, the brothers formed The Wright Cycle Company. Besides selling and repairing bicycles, the company put out two of its own models—the Van Cleve and the St. Clair.

The Wright Brothers developed a serious interest in aviation after the much-publicized death of German gliding pioneer Otto Lilienthal in 1896.

Gliders, like the one above, were critical to the development of the early planes (left) that soared over Kitty Hawk.

Lilienthal believed that by testing and studying unpowered gliders in flight, he would be able to build a motorized machine capable of sustaining flight with a pilot aboard. Curious about the challenge that Lilienthal posed, the Wrights wrote to the Smithsonian requesting every bit of available information on gliders. By 1900 they had built their own.

At the suggestion of the U.S. Weather Bureau, the Wrights chose Kitty Hawk, a remote fishing village on the Outer Banks of North Carolina, as the testing ground for their latest invention. The location's many advantages included long stretches of beach for smooth landings, winds averaging 10 to 20 mile-per-hour, and plenty of solitude for the brothers to work in secret.

In the fall of 1900, the brothers made their first journey from Dayton to Kitty Hawk to begin testing. The initial glider met with tremendous success, traveling more than 300 feet in about 20 seconds, and served as the model for an expanded 22-foot glider the following year. Although the 1901 model was the largest glider ever flown, its lift and control systems did not perform as well as the brothers' calculations had predicted.

After evaluating their progress that winter, the Wrights traced the disappointing results of the

Wilbur (left, top) and Orville (left, bottom) were not always successful in their pioneering efforts; a case in point was **the attempted flight in 1911 (above) during which Orville found himself upside down at the Flyer's controls.**

The first flight over Kitty
Hawk in 1903 (top) led to
many more successful
flights like the one above.

"The first flight lasted
only twelve seconds, a
flight modest to that of
birds, but it was, never-
theless, the first time in
the history of the world
in which a machine
carrying a man had
raised itself by its own
power into the air."
—ORVILLE WRIGHT, 1903

While most of the early flights were made over Kitty Hawk, the Wrights later took their show on the road, attracting such luminaries as King Edward VII of England (right, with beard), who traveled to Paris to watch an exhibition in 1909; most flights were as uneventful as Orville's over Fort Myer, Virginia, in 1909 (opposite page), but tragedy struck in 1908 when Lt. Thomas Selfridge (passenger above) became the airplane's first fatality after Orville's plane crashed, fracturing Selfridge's skull and severely injuring Orville.

1901 glider to a design flaw based on faulty scientific data. They spent the next several months in the back of their bicycle shop using a six-foot wind tunnel to test more than 200 wing shapes in search of the most aerodynamically sound configuration. Finally, after nearly 1,000 successful flights with the 1902 glider built from their own data, the Wright Brothers were ready to add an engine.

In just six weeks they built a 12-horsepower, 179-pound engine with which they returned to Kitty Hawk. The engine was attached to the glider and the 1903 Flyer was born.

Already disillusioned by previous unsuccessful flying attempts, only two newspapers carried the news of the Wright Brothers' historic flight. In fact, it took the Wrights years to convince the public they could fly. Not until 1908, when the brothers demonstrated a much improved version of the Wright Flyer for the U.S. War Department, did the world begin to take notice of their invention. Then it seemed everyone wanted to take a ride in the sky. As Wilbur noted, "the age of flight has come at last."

Aftermath

Although Wilbur died of typhoid in 1912, Orville lived until 1948, long enough to see the airplane change the world. In 1918, airmail was introduced in the United States. Charles Lindbergh made the first nonstop, solo, transatlantic flight in 1927. Airplanes with wingspans wider than the entire length of the Wrights' first flight played a crucial role in both World Wars. Just 66 years after the historic first flight, Neil Armstrong landed on the moon carrying a piece of cotton from the wing of the 1903 Flyer.

THE ROBIE HOUSE

Society's judgments are fickle, as even the most cursory glance at human history will attest. Were one mounting a case to prove this hypothesis, a likely first witness would be seminal twentieth century architect Frank Lloyd Wright, whose groundbreaking designs, once deemed outrageously offensive, have come to be seen as aesthetic triumphs. His beloved Robie House, begun in 1908 and considered the crowning achievement of Wright's so-called Prairie Style, is a perfect example.

An examination of the structure offers a host of reasons why Chicago's Hyde Park residents might not accept this brilliant expression of Wright's revolutionary architectural ideas. In a tree-lined neighborhood of ornate Victorian homes and the ersatz Gothic structures of the University of Chicago, Wright set out to construct a house that would reflect the vast horizontal stretches of the Midwestern prairie. Terraces merged with gardens; balconies ran the length of the house; ceilings were carried outside to roof overhangs; long, horizontal bands of limestone and brick were left unadorned. As in all of his Prairie homes, Wright was attempting to formulate a distinctively American architectural vernacular. How shocking was all this to average citizen of the day? When the Robie House was completed in 1910, neighbors called it a monstrosity, declared Wright a madman, and actually pitied the client, Frederick Robie, for having to live in such a place.

By all accounts, Robie—a forward-thinking businessman and inventor who tooled around town in an early automobile of his own design—was pleased with the house that Wright immodestly proclaimed a "cornerstone of modern architecture." It would be years before the world at large would accept the truth of that pronouncement.

The horizontal lines of the Robie House (top) allowed it to flow seamlessly into its natural surroundings (left).

> **"As for the future— the work shall grow more truly simple; more expressive with fewer lines, fewer forms; more articulate with less labor; more plastic; more fluent, although more coherent; more organic."**
> —*FRANK LLOYD WRIGHT, 1908*

Wright firmly believed that a building's architecture had a profound impact on the life and soul of those who inhabited it, a conviction that led him to develop a carefully considered design philosophy that guided his every creation. He wanted his houses to be completely "of this earth" and to blur the distinction between interior and exterior space, between the human life within and the natural world without. Toward that end, he did away with the customary hallways connecting isolated box-like rooms defined by four walls, windows and a door. Instead, the visitor to the Robie House is drawn through a succession of open, airy spaces that effortlessly flow into one another as views and light from the outside permeate the entire house. Whereas the verticality of Victorian structures seems to reflect deference to a transcendent heaven above, the Robie House, with its series of vast planes running parallel to the ground, is clearly of the here and now.

For Wright, the construction of a house was an organic process, with all the details related to one another by his overarching concept of the whole. Wright's starting point was the hearth, which he likened to the roots of a tree from which the en-tire structure must emanate, all the way to the quarter-sawn oak furniture, oak latticework screens, simple light fixtures, patterned rugs, and leaded glass doors and windows. Even the most mundane details became elements of Wright's aesthetic.

Philosophical considerations did not prevent Wright from sometimes taking into account the practicalities of everyday life. Although he would not allow the Robie family the convenience of a basement, which he viewed as an un-wholesome foundation for a house, he did design such innovative features as an attached three-car

Wright viewed the hearth (above) as the spiritual center of a house; as in many of Wright's Prairie homes, the spaces in the Robie House were connected by hallways that ran the length of the building (opposite page); for Wright, all the appurtenances were part of the aesthetic whole, including leaded glass and patterned ceilings and rugs (right).

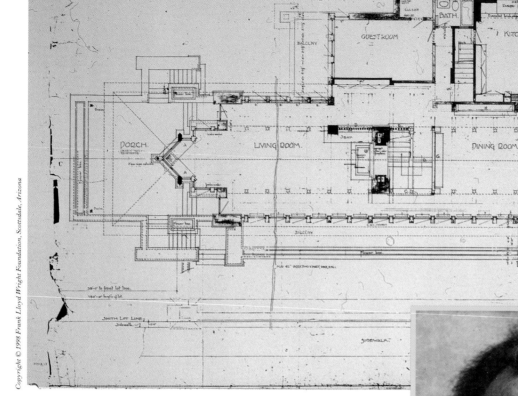

garage—perhaps the first in the country—self-watering planters, a central vacuum system, and windows that ran the length of entire walls. Furthermore, through the creation of inglenooks—smaller areas within a large room—Wright provided the Robies with places to gather as a family and, as he saw it, escape from the harsh realities of the larger world.

No level of design brilliance, however, could insulate Frederick Robie from the financial and marital difficulties that would lead him to sell the house in 1911 after living in it for only two years. When the new owners' personal misfortune landed the house back on the market less than a year later, no fewer than seven equally free-thinking prospective buyers were eager to experience life as influenced by Wright's design.

Decades after selling the house, Frederick Robie would say, "I think it's the most ideal place in the world." Indeed, this house that horrified so many who lived in the neighborhood, has since become one of the most celebrated residences of the twentieth century.

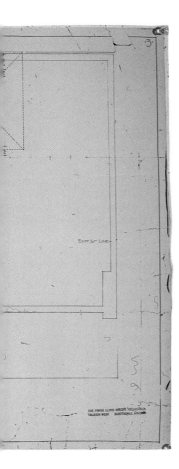

Wright (opposite page) and his design for the Robie House (left) have both taken on the status of legend; Robie (below in the backseat of an automobile of his own design) lived in the house for only two years before personal difficulties forced him to sell.

Aftermath

Having passed through a number of hands, the Robie House fell into a state of disrepair. Hyde Park residents protested once again, this time opposing plans to tear the building down. In 1963 the Robie House was donated to the University of Chicago. That year it was designated a national landmark, and the greatly needed restoration process began. The house currently serves as a home for the University of Chicago Alumni Association, but tours of the restored entry hall, living room and dining room are available to the public.

ST. LOUIS WORLD'S FAIR

From the day the St. Louis World's Fair opened on April 30, 1904 to its close seven months later, 20 million people attended, many of them more than once. The sheer size of the grounds prompted doctors to urge visitors to make several trips, since a single hurried tour would surely result in physical collapse. If some visitors did wind up in the hospital, one could understand why. Beholding a shiny new century can be shocking.

The cost of the Fair, also known as the Louisiana Purchase Exposition in honor of the centennial of the the original Louisiana Purchase, was another shock. A total of $50 million was spent erecting the main exhibition halls, while state governments, foreign nations and private exhibitors shelled out millions more to fund their own participation. (In all, some 50 countries and 45 U.S. states took part in the Fair, along with 540 concessionaires and a host of restaurants.)

Dotting the Fair's 1,200 acres and housed within six million feet of exhibit "palaces" were a cavalcade of "firsts." The Palaces of Electricity and Education, each bedecked with 24,000 lights, represented the advent of outdoor electricity use.

The waffle ice-cream cone, iced tea and hot dogs are also alleged to have made their debuts in St. Louis. George Ferris Jr.'s eponymous wheel, though not brand new—it made its debut at the Chicago World's Fair in 1893—reached a record height of 265 feet and a record capacity at 2,160 passengers. And from July to November on the fairgrounds, the United States hosted its first Olympic Games.

All of this splendor mirrored the mood of the country. The Wright Brothers had taken flight at Kitty Hawk one year earlier. Motion pictures were on the brink of a golden age, automobiles were rolling off the assembly lines and citizens increasingly were chatting on telephones. Add the

Crowds flocked through the fair gates (above) to view such exotic offerings as Missouri's Corn Temple (left).

recent U.S. victory in the Spanish-American War, and one can see why the country was brimming with hope. It seemed machinery and technology could solve any problem.

St. Louis went all out trying to prove that assertion. Among its endless exhibits were a fleet of French airships; incubators occupied by live babies; a massive working clock at the entrance to the Palace of Agriculture; an Adirondack hunting lodge replete with live beavers and fish; a recreation of the 1900 Galveston, Texas, flood; and an 18-foot lighthouse made of salt. While Brazil's display featured flowers made of bird feathers and beetle wings, Missouri contributed a 45-foot "Corn Temple," constructed of corn husks, stalks and niblets.

Not every display, however, was so innocuous. In one exhibit intended to document American

"progress" and civilization" vis-à-vis the "savage" and "primitive" peoples from other countries, scantily clad Filipinos were forced to participate in culturally inaccurate dog-eating rituals. And the Olympics featured a competition called Anthropology Days, a sporting event among "uncivilized tribes," including Pygmies, Moros,

Once the opening cere-monies (far left) were over, fairgoers were free to enjoy the world's highest Ferris wheel (left), a trip to the paint-and-plaster Tyrolean Alps (opposite page, below) or a spin in a Venetian gon-dola (below).

"There was no TV, no Disney World, no Six Flags. You could bring the world to one place and people were just amazed."

—*ROBERT ARCHIBALD,*
President & CEO,
The Missouri Historical
Society, 1996

The palatial fountain-laden grounds (above) were illumined at night by the first use of outdoor electricity (above, right); the Fair, which displayed such modern marvels as the incubator (opposite page, below) also spawned its own set of postcards such as the one at right.

Sioux, Ainu and Patagonians, who competed against one another in such events as pole-climbing, mud fighting and tug-of-war.

Such prejudice even extended to the music that accompanied many of the events. While John Philip Sousa's official Fair march, *Louisiana*, was played at concert halls throughout the month of May, a ragtime tune called *The Cascades*, written especially for the event by Scott Joplin, was barred from being performed within the fairgrounds because its composer was black.

At the close of the Fair, its Festival Hall, Colonnade of States and nearly all of its other ornate architectural confections—made of wood frames slathered with plaster of paris—were knocked down like so many stage sets. Anyone willing to pay 25 cents was allowed to watch this surreal finale to an undeniably grand spectacle. The new century was underway, warts and all.

Aftermath

Golf courses, picnic areas and tennis courts today stand where the Fair was held, along with the few structures that were saved: a birdcage at the St. Louis Zoo, a statue of King Louis IX made of plaster and dipped in bronze, and the Palace of Fine Arts—now the St. Louis Art Museum. Believed buried somewhere in St. Louis's Sterling Park are parts of the axle from the Fair's 70-ton Ferris wheel.

TEDDY BEAR

Once upon a time, there were no Teddy bears. That much is certain. How that changed and how the furry children's companion became a national craze is a source of disagreement among historians and between the German toy giant Steiff and the equally large American company the Ideal Toy Corporation.

It is generally accepted, though, that the name Teddy came from the 26th president of the United States, Theodore Roosevelt, who refused, while on a hunting trip in the Mississippi Delta, to shoot a grizzly (by some accounts a black bear cub) that had been cornered for his benefit by well-intentioned but misguided fellow hunters. The political cartoonist Clifford Berryman captured the scene for the November 18, 1902, edition of the *Washington Post* and the image of the president as a fairminded protector of innocent wildlife spread across the country. Berryman had unwittingly set in motion the rapid transformation of a vicious, temperamental animal into a symbol of innocence and affection.

Months later, Steiff introduced a plush bear to an unreceptive crowd at the 1903 Leipzig Toy Fair. Despite the lukewarm response, American toy retailer F.A.O. Schwarz placed an order for 3,000 bears—hence Steiff's claim to being first out of the gate with Teddy, although the German bear's name was Friend Petz.

Enter Morris and Rose Michtom, a Russian immigrant couple who occasionally sold handmade toys at their Brooklyn novelty store. Berryman's cartoon inspired them to make a plush bear and display it in their window with a sign saying TEDDY'S BEAR and a copy of the cartoon. When the first sold quickly, they made another, and then another, which they sent to Roosevelt, with a letter re-

Never underestimate the depth of devotion Teddy bear owners (left and above) feel for their beloved stuffed friends.

Teddies (top) were loved by boys (left) and girls (above) alike—the craze, spurred by the *Post* cartoon (far right), forced busy Teddy-makers (opposite page) to work overtime.

"When you are feeling low and desperately want to confide in someone, no one will listen more attentively than Teddy. And I am not thinking only of children."

—*PETER BULL,*
Teddy bear collector, 1984

questing permission to use his name. As the story goes, Roosevelt told them he didn't think his name would be worth much in the toy bear business, but they were welcome to use it. Soon the Michtoms began mass production. Their Ideal Toy Corporation was born, and Teddy's bear became a national, then international, hit.

In 1907 alone, Steiff sent more than 900,000 plush bears out into the world. Toy store shelves brimmed with Teddies of all shapes, sizes and abilities. Some played music, some growled. And some had eyes that lit up when their arms were raised. Ursine likenesses appeared on postcards, tea sets and paper cut-outs; and bears of means rode in specially-made automobiles, boats and trains.

The first Teddy bears were stuffed with flock clippings and old cloth and cloaked in real fur. Later generations were filled with sawdust or wood-wool and had plush wool coats. Whatever the materials, and no matter how many repairs it endured, a child's Teddy bear was often his or her most inseparable companion.

The Teddy bear's transcendence of gender

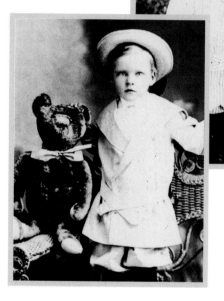

Republicans hoped that Roosevelt's close association with the Teddy bear could be transferred (opposite page) to Roosevelt's successor, William Howard Taft; in the end, kids like the ones here could not have cared less.

and socio-economic lines added to its enduring strength on the toy market, as did its ability to inspire composers, writers and poets. In 1907, American composer J.E. Bratton wrote the still-popular *Teddy Bears Picnic*. Perhaps the most famous bear of all time, Winnie-the-Pooh, born circa 1924, was inspired by the Teddy bear bought at Harrod's by author A.A. Milne's wife Dorothy for their son Christopher Robin. Another literary bear, Paddington, was Michael Bond's creative response to seeing a Teddy bear sitting all alone on a store shelf in 1956. And, in his 1960 poem *Summoned by Bells*, Sir John Betjeman waxed sentimental about his furry childhood confidante, Archibald Ormsby-Gore.

Teddy bears have also been used for less savory purposes, such as smuggling, or—when wired with a microphone—eavesdropping on a spouse. Roosevelt himself used the Teddy bear for political gain: The creature he admitted having no particular fondness for was his constant companion on the campaign trail.

ME for TAFT

Aftermath

A 20-inch Steiff Teddy bear that sold for less than a dollar in 1904, commanded $171,000 at auction in 1994 and arctophiles, or Teddy bear lovers, go by the tens of thousands to conventions to enter their well-worn bears in contests for charity prize money. The organization Good Bears of the World buys Teddies for sick children and those of any age who need support, while *The Arctophile* carries collector news and anecdotes to 10,000 subscribers around the world. Teddy bears have even been written into wills lest a bereaved bear meet an inglorious end in a tag sale, or worse, a landfill.

DINEEN, P, Boston, A

WAGNER, PITTSBURG

PHILLIPPE, PITTSBURG

YOUNG, CLEVELAND

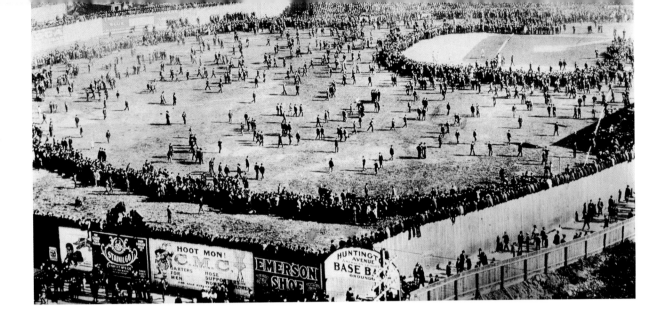

THE WORLD SERIES®

Contrary to popular myth, the game of baseball has no single inventor. The sport did not spring forth whole from the imagination of Abner Doubleday or Alexander Cartwright (to name just two of the men variously credited with being the father of the game). Rather, it evolved, with a variety of men fashioning rule changes, over the course of the nineteenth century. In the 1830s, the children's game of rounders gave way to Town Ball, which emerged as a semblance of the game we know today following the Civil War.

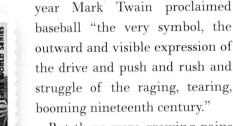

The first professional league, a slapdash affair called the National Association (N.A.), was formed in 1871. Like another American innovation soon to get off the ground, the N.A. had its own Wright Brothers, George and Harry of the Cincinnati Red Stockings, but the league was about drinking and gambling as much as pitching and hitting, and it crash-landed in 1876.

Out of the N.A.'s ashes came the National League (N.L.), which began to flourish in the 1880s, prompting the appearance of two rival circuits. Ernest Lawrence Thayer's *Casey at the Bat* entered the culture in 1888, and the following year Mark Twain proclaimed baseball "the very symbol, the outward and visible expression of the drive and push and rush and struggle of the raging, tearing, booming nineteenth century."

But there were growing pains before the game took its place as the national pastime. The 1890s saw dwindling attendance and a player revolt against management. Postseason play—though extant, with winners often billed as "champions of the world"—was fragmented by feuding between the several leagues and lack of a clear-cut format. In 1901 the rival American League (A.L.) upgraded to major-league status, clearing the way for a championship between the top two circuits. There was a way for

The series, which featured Dineen, Wagner, Phillippe and Young, ended in the Huntington Avenue Baseball Grounds (top).

Wagner (right), one of baseball's alltime greats, was hampered by injury and limited to a .222 batting average; extra seats had to be placed at field level to accommodate the crowds in Boston (left); the first Series, though not as commercial as its descendants, did generate a souvenir program (below).

SOUVENIR O▸ 10 CENTS

McGREEVY
On the Avenue
Nuff said . . . .

3rd Base

1903

..SOUVENIR CARD..

▸OF THE

World's Championship Games
Boston vs. Pittsburg

"The baseball boom of the early twentieth century built on the game's simple charms of exercise and communal celebration, adding the psychological and social complexities of vicarious play: civic pride, role models, and hero worship."

—*JOHN THORN, author, 1989*

a World Series®, but not a will. In fact, it was ill will between the N.L. and the A.L. that prevented the match from being made. When the leagues made peace in 1903, the modern World Series® games were born. Fitted with a centerpiece, America's game quickly entered its

Golden Age, ushering in names that would endure throughout the century: Ty Cobb, Christy Mathewson, Cy Young, Honus Wagner....

Wagner was conspicuous by his near absence in the 1903 Series, a best-of-nine challenge offered by Barney Dreyfuss, owner of the N.L.

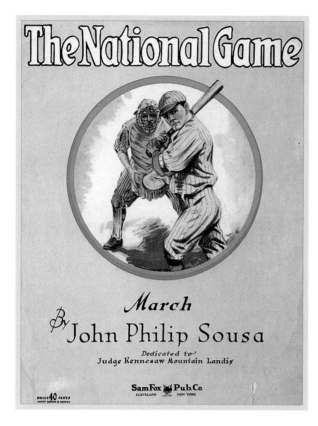

Baseball received the sure mark of cultural acceptance when John Philip Sousa composed a march in its honor (above); Pittsburgh's Dreyfuss (right) helped engineer the first series—its last game was duly recorded on the box score at far right.

champion Pittsburgh Pirates, to the Boston Pilgrims, winners of the upstart American League. The game's premier shortstop played despite an injury to his right leg, and hit just .222 while committing several errors. Wagner's injury, along with pitching ace Sam Leever's sore shoulder and hurler Ed Doheny's hospitalization for mental illness, would hamstring the favored Pirates.

With a crowd of 16,242 looking on in Boston's Huntington Avenue Baseball Grounds, the 36-year-old Young, fresh from a 28-win season, took the mound for Game 1. He was promptly touched for four runs, due in no small part to the shoddy defense of his mates. In the seventh inning, Pittsburgh's Jimmy Sebring uncorked the first World Series® home run, a solo shot to centerfield. The Pilgrims made four errors in the game and lost 7–3. They won Game 2 but Pittsburgh took Nos. 3 and 4 behind complete games from Deacon Phillippe, their only healthy starting pitcher.

Momentum shifted back to Boston in Game 5 as the Pilgrims pounded out five ground-rule triples and the great Young clamped down on the Pirates in an 11–2 rout. The Pilgrims progressed to a 5–0 lead in Game 6, holding on for a 6–3 victory that tied the Series at three games apiece.

Pittsburgh turned to Phillippe once more for Game 7. The Deacon's Sermon on the Mound again lasted nine innings, but he lost 7–3. A rainout delayed Game 8 by a day, and, with their backs against the wall, the Pirates sent Phillippe to the hill for his fifth start. He pitched valiantly, giving up just three runs, but his teammates could not solve Boston ace Bill Dineen, who twirled a four-hit shutout, delivering the first World Series® championship to Beantown.

The Pilgrims, who would be known variously as the Puritans, Plymouth Rocks, Speed Boys or Somersets before fixing on the Red Sox, would enjoy great success in the next two decades. The rest of their century, as any Bostonian will tell you, has not proved so fruitful.

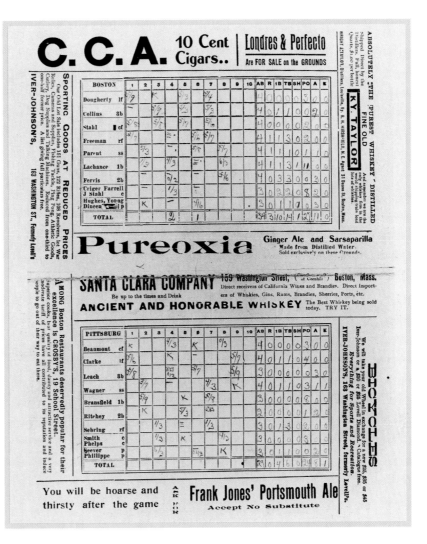

Aftermath

In 1904, John McGraw, manager of the NL champion New York Giants, refused to play the Pilgrims, who had repeated as AL titlists, saying, "We are champions of the only real major league." McGraw's crankiness caused a one-year Series hiatus, not to be repeated until the dread strike year 1994. Cy Young, who won a record 511 games in his career—arguably the most unassailable mark in sports—was 2–1 with a 1.85 ERA in the first Series. Hall-of-Famer Honus Wagner, the Flying Dutchman, hit .327 for his career and won a record eight NL batting titles.

INDEX

Adams, Samuel Hopkins 7, 51, 53, 54
American League 91
Anthropology Days 80
Archibald, Robert 81
Arctophile, The 89
Armstrong, Neil 71
Ash Can Artists 6, 11, 12, 13, 14, 15
Assembly line 5, 39, **43**
Atlas, Charles 23

Beadnell, William 35
Bellows, George 11, 12, 13, 14, 15
Berlin, Irving 23
Berryman, Clifford 85
Betjeman, John 88
Binney, Edwin 57
Binney & Smith 57, 59
Bok, Edward 53
Bond, Michael 88
Boston Pilgrims 94, 95
Bratton, J.E. 88
Bull, Peter 86
Bureau of Immigration 26

Cartwright, Alexander 91
Casey at the Bat 81
Cobb, Ty 92
Colbert, Claudette 23
Collier's 29, **54**
Czolgosz, Leon 9
Crayola crayons **56**, 57, **58**, **59**
Crisis, The 62, **64**

Davies, Arthur B. 12
Dineen, Bill **90**, 95
Doheny, Ed 94
Doubleday, Abner 91
Du Bois, W.E.B. 7, **60**, **61**, **62**, **63**, 64, **65**
Dreyfuss, Barney 92, **94**

Eastwood, Clint 37
Edison, Thomas 35
Edward VII, King **70**
Ellis, Samuel 23
Ellis Island 6, **23**, 24, **25**, 26, **27**

F.A.O. Schwarz 85
Ferris, George, Jr. 79
Ferris Wheel 79, **81**, 83
Food and Drug Administration 51
Ford, Henry 5, **38**, 39, 40
Ford Motor Company 5, 43

General Motors 43
Gibson, Charles Dana 29, **31**
Gibson girl **28**, **29**, **30**, 31
Glackens, William 10, 11, 14
Great Train Robbery, The **32**, 34, **35**, 37
Griffith, D.W. 37

Hanna, Mark 5
Harper's 29, 51
Henri, Robert 11, 14
Hope, Bob 23
Huntington Avenue Baseball Grounds **91**, 94
Hyde Park (Chicago) 73, 77

Ideal Toy Corporation 85, 87
immigrants 6, **7**, **22**, 23, 24, **25**, 26

Jazz Singer, The 37
Jolson, Al 37
Joplin, Scott 82
Jungle, The 6, 54

Kazan, Elia 23
King, Martin Luther, Jr. 64
Kitty Hawk, N.C. 5, **66**, **67**, 68, **69**, 70, 71, 79

La Follette, Robert 7
Ladies Home Journal 54
Lawson, Ernest 12
Leever, Sam 94
Life 29
Lilienthal, Otto 67
Lindbergh, Charles 71
Louisiana Purchase Exposition 79
Luks, George 11, 12, 13, 14

Malcolm X 64
Mathewson, Christy 92
McGraw, John 95
McKinley, William 9, 18
Méliès, Georges 33
Michtom, Morris and Rose 85, 87
Milne, A.A. 88
Milne, Dorothy 88
Milne, Christopher Robin 88
Model T **5**, **38**, **39**, **40**, **41**, **42**, **43**
Mt. Rainier **45**
Mt. Rushmore 21
Muir, John 9, **44**, 46, **47**, 48, **49**
Muckrakers 7, 51, 53, 54, **55**

National Association (baseball) 91
National League 91
NAACP 7, 62
National Academy of Design 12
National Park Service 45
New York Giants (baseball) 95
New York Harbor 23
New York Realists 12
Niagara Movement 61, **63**

Olympic Games, 1904 79
Ormsby-Gore, Archibald 88

Paddington Bear 88
Panama Canal 9, 20
Pan-American Exposition, Buffalo 9
patent medicines 7, **50**, **53**, 54
Pennsylvania Academy of Fine Arts 11
Pennsylvania Station **14**
Petrified Forest 45
Phillippe, Deacon 95
Pittsburgh Pirates 94, 95
Porter, Edwin S. 33, 35, **37**
Prairie Style 73
Prendergast, Maurice 12
Progressivism 7, 51
Progressive (Bull Moose) Party 17, 21
Pure Food and Drugs Act 7, 51, 55

Robie, Frederick 73, **77**
Robie House, The **72**, **73**, **74**, **75**, **76**, 77
Roosevelt, Theodore 8, 9, **16**, **17**, **18**, **19**, **20**, **21**, **44**, 49, 55, 85, 88
Rough Riders 9, 18

St. Louis Art Museum 83

St. Louis World's Fair 4, 5, 57, **78**, **79**, **80**, **81**, **82**, **83**
San Juan Hill 9, 18
Scribners 29
Sebring, Jimmy 95
Selfridge, Thomas **70**
Shinn, Everett 11, 14
Sierra Club 48, 49
Sinclair, Upton 6, 54, **55**
Sloan, John 11, 14
slums, New York City 6
Smith, Harold 57
Snyder, Robert W. 12
Sousa, John Philip 82, 94
Spanish-American War 9, 18, 80
Square Deal 9
Stamps
  1903 World Series 91
  1904 St. Louis World's Fair 79
  1906 Pure Food and Drugs Act 51
  Ash Can Painters 11
  Crayola Crayons 1903 57
  Gibson Girl 29
  Immigrants Arrive 23
  John Muir, Preservationist 45
  Kitty Hawk 1903 67
  Model T Ford 39
  President Theodore Roosevelt 17
  Robie House, Chicago 73
  "Teddy" Bear Created 85
  "The Great Train Robbery" 1903 33
  W.E.B. Du Bois, Social Activist 61
Steiff 85, 89

Taft, William Howard 9, 21
Teddy bear **84**, **85**, **86**, **87**, **88**, **89**
Thayer, Ernest Lawrence 91
Thorn, John 92
Twain, Mark 91

U.S. Dept. of Agriculture 7, 51
U.S. Dept. of Commerce and Labor 9
U.S. Public Health Service 24

Valentino, Rudolph 23
Vida, Anna 25

Wagner, Honus **90**, 92, 94, 95
War of 1812 17
Washington, Booker T. 7, 61
Washington Post 85, 87
White, William Allen 53
Whitman, Walt 12
Wiley, Harvey W. 7, **51**, **52**, 55
Wilson, Woodrow 7, 21
Winnie-the-Pooh 88
World Series®, 1903 **91**, **92**, 93, 94, 95
World War I 14, 31
Wright, Frank Lloyd 73, 74, **76**
Wright, George 91
Wright, Harry 91
Wright, Orville 67, **68**, 69, **70**, 71
Wright, Wilbur 67, **68**, 69, 71
Wright Brothers 5, 67, 71, 79
Wright Flyer, 1903 67, **69**, 71

Yellowstone Park 21, **47**
Young, Cy **90**, 92, 94, 95
Yosemite **44**, 46, **48**, 49

Ziegfeld Follies 31